curious about

BASKING SHARKS

BY MONIKA DAVIES

AMICUS LEARNING

What are you

curious about?

CHAPTER THREE

Life in the Ocean

Curious About is published by
Amicus Learning, an imprint of Amicus
P.O. Box 227, Mankato, MN 56002
www.amicuspublishing.us

Editor: Ana Brauer
Series Designer: Kathleen Petelinsek
Book Designer and Photo Researcher: Sara Hood

Library of Congress Cataloging-in-Publication Data
Names: Davies, Monika, author.
Title: Curious about basking sharks / by Monika Davies.
Description: Mankato, MN : Amicus Leawrning, an imprint of Amicus, [2026] | Series: Curious about sharks | Includes bibliographical references and index. | Audience: Ages 6–9 | Audience: Grades 2–3 | Summary: "Why do basking sharks swim with their mouths open? Learn about these giant ocean animals in this question-and-answer book for elementary-aged readers. Includes infographics, table of contents, glossary, books and websites for further research, and index"— Provided by publisher.
Identifiers: LCCN 2024048312 (print) | LCCN 2024048313 (ebook) | ISBN 9798892005012 (library binding) | ISBN 9798892005555 (paperback) | ISBN 9798892006095 (ebook)
Subjects: LCSH: Basking shark—Juvenile literature.
Classification: LCC QL638.95.C37 D38 2026 (print) | LCC QL638.95.C37 (ebook) | DDC 597.3—dc23/eng/20241207
LC record available at https://lccn.loc.gov/2024048312
LC ebook record available at https://lccn.loc.gov/2024048313

Photo Credits: Alamy Stock Photo/Alex Mustard / 2020VISION / Nature Picture Library, 11, Alex Mustard/Nature Picture Library, 10, Charles Hood, cover, 1, Dan Burton, 2, 6, Wild Wonders of Europe / Sá, 3, 16–17, 20; Blue Planet Archive/Jonathan Bird, 21; IBSG/Emmett Johnston, 18, Simon Berrow, 19; Minden Pictures/Alex Mustard / 2020VISION, 7, Chris Gomersall, 2, 14, 8; Shutterstock/berkah jaya material, 13, Chase D'animulls, 13, Choksawatdikorn, 13, Martin Prochazkacz, 4–5, wordspotrayal, 9; The Noun Project/Phạm Thanh Lộc, 22, 23, Uswa KDT, 22, visual language, 23; Vecteezy/om1947, 15

Printed in India

CHAPTER ONE

Why are they called basking sharks?

Basking sharks can live up to 50 years.

In the summer, you might spy basking sharks on the ocean's surface. They seem to 'bask' or float under the sun. That's how they got their name! Basking sharks are slow and steady giants.

A basking shark usually swims with its mouth open.

Can I swim with one?

Yes! They are calm fish. You could swim next to one. Give them space, though. These sharks have rough and sharp skin. Basking sharks swim in the Atlantic and Pacific oceans. They can also be found in the Mediterranean Sea.

Basking sharks are harmless to humans.

How big is a basking shark?

Basking sharks are also called elephant sharks because of their size.

Basking sharks are the world's second-largest fish! Only whale sharks stretch longer than them. Some basking sharks can grow up to 36 feet (11 meters) long. Most are 23 to 30 feet (7 to 9 m) long.

COMPARING SIZES

A basking shark is about the same length as a school bus!

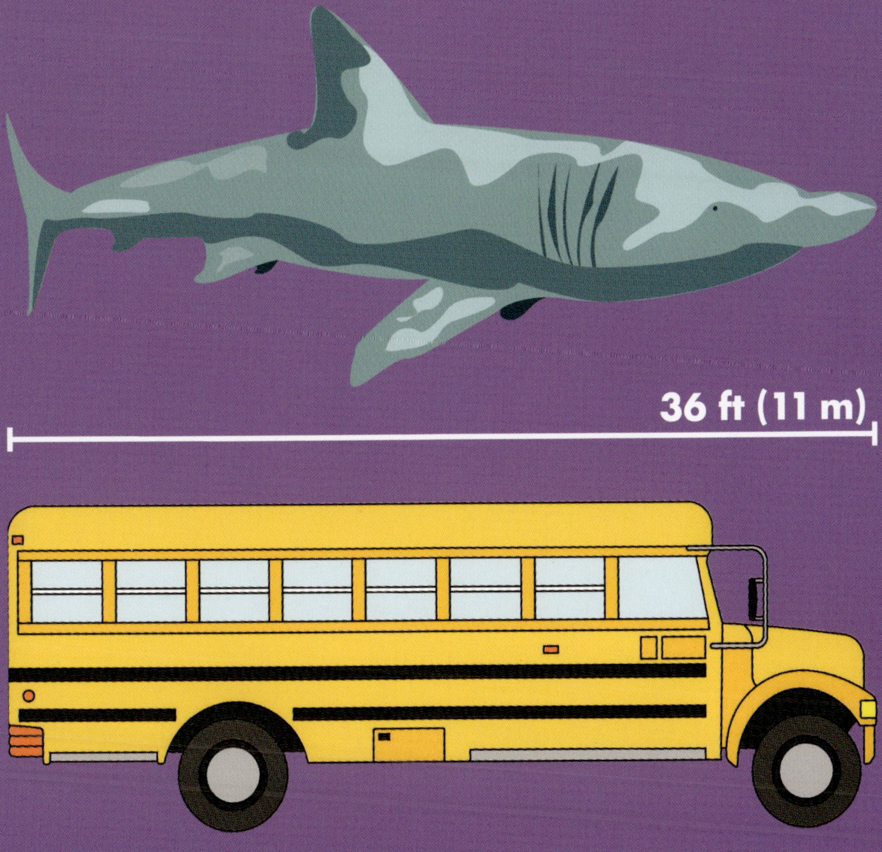

CHAPTER TWO

How do basking sharks eat?

Gill rakers help the shark catch tiny animals in the water.

Basking sharks are **filter** feeders. They eat with their mouth wide open. Food and seawater flow into their mouth. Their **gill rakers** then **divide** out the food. Then—gulp!—the sharks swallow the tiny ocean animals.

DID YOU KNOW?

Every hour, a basking shark filters about 2,000 tons (1,814 metric tons) of seawater. That's equal to over 480,000 gallons (1,816,998 liters) of milk!

Basking sharks swim with their mouths open so they can catch more food.

What do basking sharks eat?

Most often, they eat plankton. Plankton are tiny plants and animals that live in the sea. Every day, basking sharks must eat millions of plankton to live! The sharks also eat **larvae** and fish eggs.

Basking sharks mostly eat tiny animals called plankton.

DID YOU KNOW?

Plankton are often the size of a paperclip or quarter!

Basking sharks can often be seen just under the surface of the water.

Do basking sharks stay in one place?

No, basking sharks are **migratory.** They move from sea to sea. They travel in search of plankton. The sharks stay to the north in the summer. They move to the south in the winter.

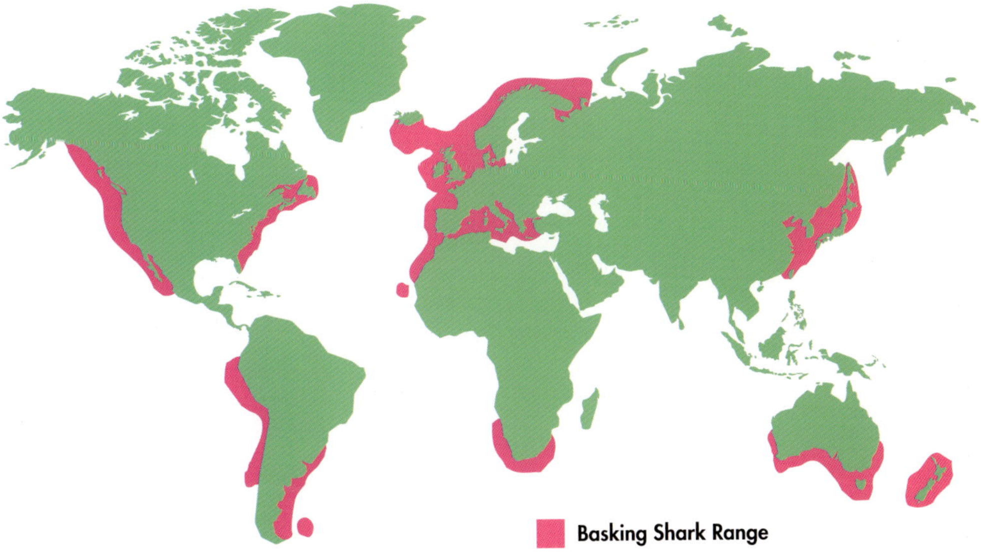

How are basking shark babies born?

The answer is a bit of a mystery! Baby basking sharks grow inside eggs. These eggs are inside the mother shark. But the sharks **hatch** in the mother's womb. Their babies are then born live.

DID YOU KNOW?

A baby basking shark might take over three years to grow inside its mother.

Young basking sharks are left behind after birth. They must find food alone.

Do basking sharks swim together?

Basking sharks are social creatures.

Sometimes! Basking sharks often swim alone. But they also swim in pairs. The sharks sometimes travel as a family. You might even see a large group swimming together during mating season.

During mating season, basking sharks will swim in large circles. Scientists are not fully sure why.

Are basking sharks endangered?

Basking sharks are hunted for their meat and fins.

Yes. The number of basking sharks is low. Basking sharks are slow and gentle creatures. This makes them easier to catch. Humans hunt them sometimes. There are now laws against hunting or catching basking sharks. These laws keep them safe.

Basking sharks swim about 2.3 miles (3.7 kilometers) per hour.

ASK MORE QUESTIONS

Where is the best place to see basking sharks?

Do basking sharks have any other names?

Try a BIG QUESTION: How can humans take care of basking sharks?

SEARCH FOR ANSWERS

Search the library catalog or the Internet.
A librarian, teacher, or parent can help you.

Using Keywords
Find the looking glass.

Keywords are the most important words in your question.

If you want to know about:

- where to find basking sharks, type: BASKING SHARK LOCATIONS
- other names for basking sharks, type: BASKING SHARK NAMES

LEARN MORE

FIND GOOD SOURCES

Here are some good, safe sources you can use in your research.
Your librarian can help you find more.

Books

Basking Sharks
by Jennifer Boothroyd, 2022.

Basking Sharks
by Rebecca Pettiford, 2021.

Internet Sites

Britannica Kids | Basking Shark
https://kids.britannica.com/kids/article/basking-shark/639026
Britannica Kids has fact-checked articles about many different animals.

National Geographic Kids | Surprising Sharks
https://kids.nationalgeographic.com/animals/fish/article/surprising-sharks
Learn more about other surprising species of sharks.

Every effort has been made to ensure that these websites are appropriate for children. However, because of the nature of the Internet, it is impossible to guarantee that these sites will remain active indefinitely or that their contents will not be altered.

SHARE AND TAKE ACTION

Most people think sharks are scary! But basking sharks are gentle creatures.
Share what you have learned with your friends.

The plastic in our oceans hurts sea creatures. Find ways to use less plastic.
Bring a cloth bag for shopping. Use a reusable water bottle.

Help take care of the oceans for basking sharks. Do not throw garbage in the ocean.
Join a beach clean-up. Try to use less water.

GLOSSARY

divide To separate something into two or more parts.

filter Something that is used to remove something from a liquid, like seawater, that passes through it.

gill rakers Thin, bony body parts that catch tiny food items, like plankton.

hatch To be born by coming out of an egg.

larvae The wormlike form of an animal that hatches from an egg.

migrate To move from one place to another.

INDEX

About the Author

Monika Davies is a Canadian author of over 60 books for young readers. She thinks sharks are fascinating—and hopes you agree! When Monika isn't writing, you can find her strolling by the ocean, reading books too quickly, or trying to keep her seven plants alive.